Real estate investment tips

How to sell in real estate

JAMES RICK

Real estate investment tips

Real estate investment tips

Table of contents

Chapter 1

Real estate.

Real estate investing is the practice of buying a piece of real estate as an investment rather than living in it. It can be simply defined as any tangible asset that is typically immobile yet transferable, such as a piece of land, a building, infrastructure, or any tangible asset.

A house, an office building, a piece of land used for agriculture or a business, etc. are some examples of real estate. It is thought regarded as a safe form of investment.

Property Investing Features
When it comes to real estate, we can say that it takes a lot of foresight and financial investment to anticipate profitable returns.

Real estate investment tips

Now let's look at each of the qualities of real estate investment individually.

Tangible: One of those assets that have a tangible reality and can be touched and seen is real estate or properties. Investment in real estate is a wise choice when economic inflation harms the value of other investments. It is the only investment that generates a value appraisal when things go wrong. Financial institutions are drawn to funding for real estate because of its physical existence and ability to be used as leverage.

Uncertain Maturity Period: Unlike other types of investments, such as fixed deposits and bonds, real estate investments do not have a set maturity period. The owner chooses whether to keep or sell the property.

Value Enhancement: Purchasing real estate can benefit investors in two different ways.

Real estate investment tips

Real estate creates rental income on the one hand, while at the same time, over time, its value keeps rising.

Low Liquidity: Real estate's status as a capital asset is one of its fundamental characteristics. It cannot, therefore, be routinely purchased or sold like stocks or equities.

Needs Management: Investing in real estate entails purchasing a tangible asset and incurring upkeep costs. The source of income thus produced must also be managed by the investor.

Universal Acceptance as Collateral: Taking real estate as collateral to finance loans is a standard practice among banks and other financial organizations.

Profitable Even During Recession: Historically, real estate has been regarded as one of the safest investment options. Even during a recession, if done properly, they can produce money or profit.

Advantages of real estate investment

Long-term benefits of investing in real estate are possible. It might produce significant rewards if done carefully. The following are some benefits of investing in real estate together:

Invest in Real Estate as an Inflation Hedger: Unlike other assets, real estate is not negatively impacted by inflation. Instead, as the economy grows, so do its value and income. Only residential and commercial properties can generate enough money from rentals to pay down the principal and interest on their mortgage. The major source of creating passive income is a stable income. To guarantee a consistent and constant flow of cash, the investors can rent out their homes.

Real estate investment tips

Tax advantages: Real estate investors enjoy tax exemptions on rental income up to a certain threshold. Even the tax rates are quite low for such investments when done over the long term. Real estate investors have the same freedom to choose their actions as they would with any other type of business. In essence, the investor is the employee's boss.

Financial stability: As we all know, investing in real estate requires patience. A physical asset is in the investor's hands, which gives the personal financial security.

Value Appreciation: Purchasing real estate involves investing in assets that will eventually experience capital growth.

Disadvantages of Real Estate Investing

Real estate has various restrictions, which are covered below, even when it is a good investment:

High Maintenance and Management: Buying real estate as an investment entails paying for the upkeep of a physical asset. The source of income thus produced must also be managed by the investor.

Large Transaction Cost: Purchasing and selling properties is an expensive endeavor. Because of the high transaction costs, which include registration fees, legal fees, diverting business, and other costs, the buyer's cost of investment rises.

Creates Legal and Financial Liability: If an investor purchases a property with a loan, the investor may be left with an excessive financial liability. Investors are subject to legal obligations even when ownership is transferred at the moment of property purchase.

Less Liquid: Real estate can be more difficult to buy and sell often than other investments like equities. Because of this, it might not be a good choice for investors looking for quick returns.

Dealing with Market Inefficiencies: Investors who lack the requisite knowledge about a potential real estate project can pool their funds towards less profitable enterprises. Real estate appraisals do not occur at a fixed rate or over a predetermined length of time. Property capital gains are a long-term process; they are presumptive but not predetermined.

Real estate investing reasons for failure

Real estate investing, if not done carefully, may potentially result in subpar returns or a decline in the property's value. The following are some of the main reasons why real estate investing fails:

Lack of knowledge: Before making a real estate investment, one should be

Real estate investment tips

well-versed in all aspects of the venture. Most investors don't consider the potential of the property or the best moment to invest, which prevents them from getting significant returns on their money.

Poor Management: Purchasing an appropriate home or real estate project as an investment requires skill. However, the investor must give equal consideration to the management and upkeep of that property, contractors, budget, and renters. The returns could decrease in the case of real estate that is not well managed.

False Calculation: To calculate a project's potential profitability in real estate investing, you need to have a calculative mindset and solid arithmetic abilities. Investors occasionally fall short in these specific areas and support less advantageous ventures.

Real estate investment tips

Giving Up Too Soon: One of the biggest mistakes impatient investors make is anticipating a quick and substantial return on their real estate investment. And if it doesn't, they quickly lose hope and give up. These people need to understand that these investments have substantial long-term returns.

Chapter 2

Forms of Real Estate Investment

Real estate is one of the most popular investments because, if you play your cards right, it has a lot of advantages. However, learning about all the various types of investments you have available to you when you're just starting in real estate investing can be a little overwhelming. The first step is to understand the different kinds of real estate investments and how they operate. Here are some things you should know before choosing where to invest your money.

Real estate investment types: understanding them.

Real estate investment tips

The first thing that comes to mind when thinking about real estate investing might be purchasing an investment property and renting it out. While this is a viable option, it is only a small portion of the real estate investment options available to you. The majority of real estate investments can be divided into one of two categories: active or passive. Active investments require you to invest not only your money but also, possibly, your time and physical labor. Active investing includes activities like managing residential rental properties and flipping homes because they both demand a lot of work from the investor. In general, active investments are slightly more profitable than passive ones, but at a cost of higher cost and generally higher risk.

Real estate investments can be made in passive ways, which frequently don't require you to personally own or manage a property. Passive investment strategies include crowdfunding, real estate investment trusts

Real estate investment tips

(REITs), and real estate funds. These techniques enable you to invest in real estate without having to make a sizable upfront financial commitment or manage any properties. There are many ways to start investing in real estate, regardless of whether you have the time or money to dedicate to a rental property. Let's take a look at a few of your options.

1. Home-based Real Estate

Most people are familiar with and understand residential real estate as a real estate investment. Having said that, there are numerous distinct residential real estate investment strategies that you may or may not be aware of, ranging from micro-flipping to accessory dwelling units (ADUs). Residential real estate investments are typically active, so you'll probably need to put in a lot of time and money to make them work. However, they have the potential to yield sizable profits and steady cash flow.

Real estate investment tips

Investments in Residential Real Estate:
Let's look at some of your options since investing in residential real estate can be many different things. Renting for a while A long-term rental property is a piece of land that you purchase with the intent to lease to tenants. From a small, single-family home to a multifamily building with up to four units, this property can be of any type. The rent you receive from tenants and/or the increased value of the property if you decide to sell the property in the future is how you as an investor profit from these kinds of properties. It is not necessary by any means, but some investors choose to live on-site at the rental property they are managing, which is referred to as an owner-occupied multifamily property.

Rental property for vacations: Owning a rental property for long-term guests is similar to owning a vacation home. You purchase a home, typically in a touristy area, and then rent it out (typically on a short-term basis) to travelers who will stay there for a limited amount of time. Because you or someone who works from your home will need to constantly manage the maintenance of the property in between guests, this may be one of the more labor-intensive residential real estate investments.

One of the most active investments you can make is flipping or microflipping a house. When you flip a house, you buy a fixer-upper that requires urgent repairs, make those repairs, and then sell it. Because you have to put a lot of your own money into the house and there's a chance you'll discover new issues and lose money rather than making a profit, this is typically risky. However, everything being equal, you could stand to gain thousands of dollars from the sale. In a less extreme variation of this, called microflipping, you purchase houses that are being offered for less than their potential market value and quickly resell them, frequently without making significant repairs. While less profitable than conventional flipping, this also involves less risk and expense.

ADU: An ADU is an additional living space on your property that you rent to a tenant, usually a family member. Examples of ADUs include sheds and basements that have been converted into tiny homes. An ADU can be a good option for those looking to make some passive income from their current property because operating one is typically less expensive than managing another entire property.

Pros
If you know what you're doing, you could potentially recover a significant portion of

your investment. Your monthly income could increase significantly if you find the ideal property in the ideal location.

Over time, the value of real estate increases. You'll likely get a good return on your investment if you purchase a house, especially at a discount, make the necessary repairs, and then later sell it.

Investing in real estate has tax advantages, including tax deductions, depending on your income level.

Cons
Real estate for residential use can be very expensive to invest in. Recall that you must invest your own money in buying and renovating real estate, which can cost thousands upon thousands of dollars, especially if you're doing something like flipping a house.

Real estate investment tips

It can take a lot of time to manage real estate on your own. It can take a lot of your time to maintain the property or carry out other tasks related to being a landlord, like taking care of repairs and collecting rent.

Managing a property is not a very liquid investment, so unlike some other investment options, you cannot simply sell something quickly and withdraw money from your investment.

2. Industrial Real Estate

The term "commercial real estate" describes real estate holdings that are ordinarily not residential. Commercial real estate investments include things like hotels, warehouses, offices, and retail stores. The investor owns and rents out a space to a company that will use it in these kinds of investments, which are also frequently regarded as active investments. Similar to residential real estate, commercial real estate also allows you to generate additional

Real estate investment tips

cash flow by collecting rent or selling the asset as its value increases.

Pros

The returns from commercial real estate are generally higher than those from residential. Depending on the area you are in, managing a commercial space may prove profitable over time if you can afford it.

The amount of income a piece of commercial real estate produces plays a role in determining its value. However, if your property is home to prosperous businesses, its value may increase much more quickly than a residential property.

In comparison to residential investments, upkeep may not be as risky. Since you'll probably be renting out commercial spaces to companies, the relationships between tenant and owner tend to be more formal.

Cons

Real estate investment tips

You have to consider both the general public and your tenants when making commercial investments. To keep your property in good condition and to assist you in handling any potential problems, you might need professional assistance.

Commercial investments typically take more time as well. You'll probably need to manage several leases and more potential problems rather than just a small number of tenants.

There is more risk involved overall because your investment property is public. Commercial building investors may have greater concerns regarding someone getting hurt on the property or causing property damage than residential building owners.

3. Plain Land
A piece of property is described as being "raw land" if it has no structures, paths,

crops, or anything else on it. Undeveloped land typically costs less to invest in than developed land, and like other types of real estate, its value increases over time. A land loan can also be used to buy undeveloped land, particularly if you intend to develop it.

Many owners of raw land lease their land to farmers for agricultural use, or they look for properties with development potential to sell at a later date for a profit.

Pros
Compared to many other investments, raw land is simple to acquire. Compared to developed land, buildings, or homes, it is significantly less expensive.

The cost of maintenance is not excessive. You won't have to worry about making updates or repairs all the time, unlike managing a building.

Real estate investment tips

With raw land, you have a wide range of options. On the land you buy, you could construct something, lease it, or buy and hold it.

Cons

You receive limited tax benefits from vacant land. You won't be able to benefit from raw land the way you might from an investment in a structure with a mortgage.

You might not start off making a lot of money. If you purchase land to hold it, you may simply have to wait for it to value while keeping the option of renting it out for various uses.

Zoning can be challenging. Your investment could succeed or fail depending on the use that the land is zoned for. Furthermore, whether a property is classified for commercial or residential use, it may be challenging to obtain township clearance for any development plans you may have for the property.

4. REITs

Real estate trust investments, or REITs, are businesses that manage a variety of real estate investments while operating as trusts. REITs are regarded as passive investments, as opposed to many of the earlier possibilities. Instead of owning buildings directly, you can invest in a REIT and get income from the assets that the business manages.

Publicly traded REITs are some of those that are listed on the NYSE. A REIT can be a wonderful alternative if you're interested in commercial real estate but lack the funds to invest directly in a property. These organizations often specialize in commercial assets, such as malls, offices, and hospitals.

Pros

Real estate investment tips

You can earn extra money without ever having to visit, oversee, or own a property. When investing in something like a REIT, there is no workload associated with active real estate investments.

You can anticipate earning consistent, albeit modest, income, depending on the REIT you invest in.

Although technically stocks, many REITs have great liquidity and can help diversify your portfolio because they are real estate assets.

Cons

If you want to make a lot of money immediately, REITs won't be much help because they work best as long-term investments that provide you with increasing quantities of cash over time.

Additionally, REITs have a higher tax rate than eligible dividends.

A REIT gives you limited influence over your investments because you don't personally own or manage any of the buildings or loans.

5. Property crowdfunding

Real estate crowdfunding is a novel technique that enables individuals to pool their cash and participate in opportunities they wouldn't be able to afford on their own. Typically, this happens online. Similar to REITs, this form of investing also qualifies as passive and requires a considerably smaller initial investment.

Some online real estate crowdfunding services are accessible to all investors, but many others demand that users provide proof of a minimum amount of income.

Pros

Real estate investment tips

You may diversify your investment portfolio through crowdfunding without needing to make exorbitant sums of money.

Without the assistance of other investors online, it gives investors access to uncommon chances.

In contrast to conventional real estate investments, which could have upkeep and other maintenance fees related to owning property or land, there is relatively little effort required, and the entire process is often completed online.

Cons
Dividends received by investors in crowdfunding are taxed.

Contrary to the expectations of investors drawn to crowdsourcing by its low entrance financial bar, some investing platforms may

Real estate investment tips

require that you satisfy a minimum income
level to join.

Users of crowdfunding platforms may be
charged for using their services.

Chapter 3

Understand your competitors

Life is competitive for all of us. You're no stranger to the challenging competition as a real estate agent. Despite the challenges that competition may present, it is crucial to understand that it is a positive force for the development of the real estate sector in general and your real estate brand in particular. Realizing your skills and shortcomings as well as those of your competitors, however, is what separates you from the crowd and helps you win. Due to this, it's critical to carry out a thorough competitive study and researches any potential real estate competitors.

The foundations of competition will now be discussed. Direct and indirect competition come in two flavors. Who then are real estate agents' direct and indirect competitors?

Businesses that provide the same service as your brand are considered to be in direct rivalry. Agents in the real estate industry are so directly competing with one another. While indirect rivals don't provide the same service as their direct counterparts, they still fulfill the same demands in a different method. Services like for-sale-by-owner, for instance, can be indirect competitors of real estate brokers. Understanding your indirect competition is just as crucial as understanding your direct rivals. You learn more about the factors that influence people's decisions to use or reject your services as a result.

How to spot your competitors

After determining who your key rivals are, it's your responsibility to keep tabs on them.

Real estate investment tips

Therefore, the following are some considerations:

Real Estate Keywords

Find out the keywords they're using for both paid and organic searches. It will be easier for you to determine what keywords your rivals are weak in if you are aware of their target keywords as well as the broader trends. You can learn more about the primary keywords used by your competition by using tools like SpyFu.

Because there is so much digital content available, it can be quite challenging to surprise and engage visitors. Because of this, shared material indicates that your rivals have discovered a market that hasn't yet been fully exploited. Investigate it thoroughly and give the reason(s) for sharing this content some thought. Don't duplicate it; try to understand it.

Use Google Alerts

One of the most well-known search engine services is Google. People want to get their content to at least show up on the first page of Google, if not present there altogether. Every entrepreneur who succeeds has this as his ultimate objective. This can be accomplished with a little bit of luck, but most crucially by regularly monitoring the most recent developments in your sector and keeping an eye on the competition. To accomplish both, use Google Alerts. You may find it useful to know what other publications are saying about your rivals, what material appears when certain crucial keywords are searched, or even what others are saying about you.

One technique to identify where your SEO efforts need improvement is by looking at your backlink profile. You can identify areas where your marketing efforts need to be strengthened by knowing your backlinks and studying those of your competitors. You may assist with that by using tools like Ubersuggest, particularly SEO Explorer.

Manual examination

You should conduct manual research in addition to using certain tools to examine your competition. The simplest action to take is to search for the terms you want to rank for on Google. Verify the person taking the lead. They may be your direct or indirect competition depending on whether they do that. Look into regional searches.

To find your local competitors and improve your Google My Business page, utilize keywords like "real estate agents around me." to help you rank locally. Check out our in-depth guide to setting up a Google My Business profile for a real estate agent as well.

How to monitor your competitors and what to look out for

Social Media

One of the most crucial platforms for connecting with both current and new customers is social media. Your social media strategy will be more thorough if you are aware of the broad real estate market trends as well as how your rivals are utilizing social media.

Actual Estate Blogs

Blogging is still very popular, although consumers are increasingly drawn to visual content. Blogging helps your website get the traffic it needs while giving your readers content they can utilize. It can inspire creativity and provide you with a novel, original ideas for topics to write about. Then then, keep that in mind. Even though plagiarism is sometimes seen as a flattering act, this is not true of digital output.

Real estate investment tips

Although they can serve as an inspiration, blogs should not be verbatim copied.

Property Newsletters

Email marketing is a tried-and-true strategy for connecting with and interacting with your audience. Important messages and updates can be distributed effectively in this fashion. To observe what kinds of emails your competitors are sending, sign up for their newsletters if they have one. Additionally, it will inspire you to create a fresh newsletter campaign.

Review of Clients

You can evaluate your strengths and weaknesses and enhance your customer service by learning how your competitors interact with their customers. By being aware of the needs of your competitors' customers, you can fill that void and provide a better service.

Tools for Identifying and Tracking Your Competitors.

Ubersuggest: website traffic analysis, SEO exploration, keyword research, and more

A free option is available from Alexa for site information, which also displays the website rank and compares websites that are deemed to be rivals.

The free domain rating checker Ahrefs also displays the authority of the websites (the higher DR you have the better)

Comprehensive Keyword Analyzer SpyFu Alerts from Google Create a Google Alert for a specific set of keywords to learn what others are saying about your rivals.

Social Mention- Aids you in determining what consumers are saying about your company or your rivals on social media.

Real estate investment tips

Additionally, you may utilize Google Keyword Planner to find terms used by your rivals. Since the data is directly from Google, it is more accurate.

Semrush is an excellent additional tool for keyword research.

Chapter 4

Analyzes the market

You likely have some experience determining a property's value if you've ever bought or sold a house. The likelihood of the house selling dramatically decreases if the asking price is too high. On the other hand, if a house you want to sell is priced too low, you'll pass up the chance to make a profit.

A real estate market analysis should always be done before buying or selling a house to ensure that it is priced fairly. To determine an accurate market price, this analysis will compare the values of nearby homes that are similar to the ones under consideration. Let's define real estate market analysis first before discussing how to conduct one.

What Analysis Of The Real 1 Estate Market Is

Often referred to as comparative market analysis, a real estate market analysis (CMA). It consists of an analysis of recent property market values that are comparable to the one you want to buy or sell. If you're trying to decide on an accurate selling price before listing your home, a CMA is a useful tool for figuring out the market value of your property.

A real estate market analysis differs from an appraised value, which is established by a qualified appraiser, which is something to keep in mind. The seller is provided with information on the value of nearby homes with the help of a comparable market analysis, which is regarded as subjective. Even though there are many factors to consider when conducting a real estate

Real estate investment tips

market analysis, it is completely manageable with a well-planned strategy.

To help you decide what to list your home for sale or what to offer for a home, your real estate agent may perform a CMA. Adjustments must be made to take into account differences because no two properties are exactly alike.

Reasons for Conducting a Real Estate Market Analysis

No matter if you are buying or selling a home, you should always conduct a real estate market analysis. This analysis will assist you in comprehending the current housing market, the value of properties similar to yours, and, if it's an investment property, the rent you can command.

The data gathered from a real estate market analysis, also known as a CMA, aid buyers in determining whether an asking price is reasonable, too high, or too low. A CMA should always be performed to ensure that, based on the value of the property, both buyers and sellers are receiving a fair deal.

You can determine an exact price for a home by evaluating comparable listings on the market.

How to Conduct an Analysis of the Real Estate Market.

Initial Property Analysis
Perform a property analysis as the first step in your real estate market analysis. It is important to assess the following qualities:

Area and neighborhood: Check out the neighborhood where the property is located by driving around. Use online tools like Google Street View when looking at a property that is located out of your state to determine which streets or neighborhoods are nicer than others. It may be challenging

Real estate investment tips

to tell how nice the neighborhood is because Google's images could be outdated.

Dimensions or square footage.

Measurement of the lot.

Bedrooms and bathrooms: The number of bedrooms and bathrooms is crucial in determining a home's value. Two bedrooms, for example, are less desirable than three or more. Furthermore, houses with just one bathroom typically fetch less money when they are put on the market.

Other spaces: It's a good idea to check to see if spaces that may have been used as an office or den would qualify as a bedroom because homes with more bedrooms typically cost more to buy. To determine whether other rooms can legitimately be categorized as bedrooms, check your local building codes.

Real estate investment tips

Quantity of floors.
The age of the building, including when it was built, renovated, expanded, etc., affects how much a property is worth. Unless preserving an ancient home's antiquity or original architecture is regarded as desirable in the neighborhood, newer residences will be valued higher.

The value of the property may be increased by some amenities and features, such as a fireplace, deck, garden, swimming pool, balcony, etc. Other features can include the house being in a gated neighborhood with a clubhouse or having access to tennis courts. The home's value is influenced by each of these factors.

Consider the property's proximity to busy roads, rapid freeway access, stores, public transportation, parks, schools, and other neighborhood amenities. Check to discover if a property is adjacent to any unwanted locations, such as a landfill or commercial buildings.

New or noteworthy developments.

2. Determine the Original List Price

After you've completed the property study, try to find the original listing online. You'll get a decent idea of the home's general condition from this. Look over the images and descriptions for any alterations, remodels, or potential problems. To tell whether the house was custom-made or a prefabricated one, the builder or developer needs also to be included.

3. Examine estimates of property values

Use internet tools like Zillow Zestimates to determine the home's estimated market worth. Since they are just estimates, especially if the home has undergone renovations, they might not be entirely accurate. However, this will provide you with an excellent baseline figure to work from as you continue to analyze the real estate market.

4. Search Comps
The following stage is to look for homes that are similar to yours. Comparable houses ought to have the same number of bedrooms and bathrooms, be less than 300 square feet in size, be situated in the same neighborhood, have a comparable lot size, and be similar in terms of the house's age and features.

Look out for Recently Sold Properties in the Area.

You may find out just how much comparable properties in the region are sold by searching online for sold listings. Analyze previous postings that are between one and three miles from your property. Since market trends change, look for properties that have recently sold as this will provide you with the most accurate valuation. If more information is needed, extend your search to the last six months. To your list of comps, add three to five comparable properties.

Browse current comparable home listings. Search for recent listings of comparable houses in a one- to the three-mile area after that. Pick at least three residences that are comparable to yours. Remember that these listing prices may not be accurate representations of the market. A sellers' market typically tries to inflate values by pricing more, whereas a buyers' market typically tries to deflate values by charging less. Real estate trends have an impact on unsold homes' value. You may get a decent understanding of your competitors' characteristics by looking at current postings.

Take into account pending listings for comparable homes. Even if pending listings have not yet been fully closed, looking at

Real estate investment tips

them will give you current information about the market's state.

Examine expired listings for comparable properties. The last thing you should check is expired postings for comparable properties. Because homes that have expired typically had overpriced asking prices, this information is incredibly helpful for your market study.

5. Choose a price range
It's time to decide on a price range for your house now that you have a list of all the relevant details.

Set Your Ceiling Value
Choose a property that is unquestionably worth more than yours out of the three to five comparable properties you found. The home can be newer, be in a better neighborhood, or have more features. This amount will serve as your pricing range's upper limit or ceiling value.

Establish Your Floor Price
Select a home next that is unquestionably worth less than yours. It can be in a congested area, have fewer amenities, or have less appealing curb appeal. Your floor price, often known as your price range's low point, will be this amount.

6. Examine the House Directly
If at all possible, evaluate a home personally as there is no more accurate approach to determine its pricing. When touring the property, make a note of elements that will affect value, such as the general state, any alterations or improvements, amenities, features, any repairs or improvements that are required, as well as the exterior and landscaping.

7. Establish Market Value
You ought to have an idea of the price range your property is worth based on all of your research. Consider the impact on the value

Real estate investment tips

of everything you noticed while strolling through the house. After that, divide the selling prices of the comparable homes on your list by their square footage to determine the price per square foot for each one of them. The average price per square foot of your comparable sales should be multiplied by the number of square feet in the house you are seeking to sell or buy.

Last but not least, choose where your home fits inside the predetermined price range. This figure represents your home's market value.

Example of Average Price From Comps Calculation.

To assist you in estimating average prices from comparable listings, here is an example of comparative market analysis (CMA).

Real estate investment tips

Suppose your property is 2,500 square feet, and after study, you have found five comparable homes:

2,700 square foot house with a $490,000 sale price (or $181 per square foot)

Home number two was 3,000 square feet in size and sold for $510,000 ($170 per square foot).

Housing unit three was 2,200 square feet and sold for $455,000 ($206 per square foot).

Property number four was 2,400 square feet and sold for $475,000 ($197 per square foot).

Property number five was 2,650 square feet and sold for $485,000 ($183 per square foot).

Real estate investment tips

These five comparable houses cost $187.40 on average per square foot. Then increase the square footage of your property (2,500) by the typical price per square foot ($187.40), which results in a rough estimate of the home's value of $468,500. This is a fairly realistic estimation of the asking price for your house.

Learning how to do your real estate market analysis may seem like a difficult task. But if you adhere to our step-by-step instructions, you'll be able to calculate an exact property price for any real estate venture. To be sure you aren't overpricing your house as a seller, perform a real estate market analysis. Expiring listings and a loss of market freshness are the results of overpricing. The more money you stand to lose the longer your house is on the market. Alternatively, if you overvalue your home, you risk losing out on prospective revenue. To get your home's most accurate market value, use free web resources.

Chapter 5

Investment tactics for Real Estate

Real estate ownership can be a useful method to diversify an investment portfolio by adding security that produces returns comparable to those of the stock market but with less volatility. Investors can employ leverage to increase overall profits, and residential real estate offers special tax incentives to investors. Although physically owning investment properties is the most typical kind of real estate investment, there are many other ways that investors hope to profit from real estate. These real estate investing tactics are employed by both novice and experienced investors. Different tactics will perform better for you than others in real estate investing, based on your goals and periods.

1. Invest in and hold real estate

A real estate investment strategy utilized to generate rental income, profit from long-term property value growth, and take advantage of certain tax advantages available to real estate investors is the purchase and holding of SFR properties. SFR real estate is undoubtedly the most well-liked investment option for both novice and experienced investors. SFRs makeup 35% of all rental properties in the nation, according to Green Street, an independent real estate research and advising business, in its most recent U.S. Single-Family Rental Outlook study.

Finding, owning, and operating SFRs might be fairly simple. Residential real estate can be financed in a variety of ways, from conventional and government-backed loans to private and portfolio lenders. Almost the past 20 years, the median sales price of houses sold in the United States has climbed by over 200%, while the demand for rental property has not decreased. However, due to upkeep, repairs, or prospective vacancies, net income from rental property may vary, and some investors may favor a more passive approach to investing.

2. Invest rental revenue

Many buy-and-hold real estate investors employ reinvesting rental income as a supplemental strategy. Net cash flow from one rental property is saved up until enough money is available for the down payment on a second rental property, a strategy often known as the "snowball effect." After that, the net cash flow from both rental properties is preserved until there is enough money to purchase a third rental property. Similar to a snowball rolling down a slope, as an investor's portfolio of rental properties grows, so does the snowball of income earned.

Some property owners additionally reinvest rental revenue by making extra mortgage payments to pay off a mortgage on a piece of property more quickly. A cash-out refinance is carried out by the investor to convert accumulated equity into cash so that it can be used to buy another rental property whenever there is sufficient equity created by appreciation and mortgage prepayments.

3. Home invasion

The possibility of needing a sizable sum of money for a down payment is one disadvantage of investing in rental property. People who own their home but lack the additional finances to buy a rental property use the real estate investing approach known as "house hacking." Renting out an extra bedroom or turning a basement into a studio apartment are two examples of house hacking. Up until there is enough money for a down payment on a rental property, rental income from house hacking is kept.

Some investors will house-hack by obtaining a modest, multifamily property with a minimal down payment through a Federal Housing Administration (FHA) or Veterans Affairs (VA) loan. This method has the potential disadvantage that the borrower must occupy one of the apartments as their principal residence. A great approach to learning about real estate investing and obtaining practical property management experience is, however, to live next door to tenants.

4. BRRRR

Real estate investors employ the buy, remodel, rent, refinance, repeat (BRRRR) approach to purchase fixer-upper properties utilizing short-term financing, perform any necessary renovations, lease to a qualifying tenant, then refinance and withdraw cash after the property has a stable history of positive cash flow. Similar to the snowball effect, the BRRRR real estate investing technique involves an investor doing the same thing repeatedly. BRRRR is typically a preferable plan for an active investor who has the time and expertise to complete tasks on their own or has a reliable, cost-efficient network of contractors and handypeople to assist in remodeling. An investor must be careful not to run out of money until the property starts to cash flow because one disadvantage of BRRRR is that short-term financing frequently involves high loan fees and interest rates.

5. Repair and conversion

If all goes according to plan, house flipping is a high-risk real estate investing method that could provide a sizable profit. Fix-and-flip investors don't want to be landlords because they only intend to own a property for a brief period. A flipper who finds and buys an undervalued property may decide to hold onto the property and hope for appreciation in value, or they may choose to undertake strategic improvements to boost the value of the property. Investors may run out of money if they are unable to flip a house quickly or if they underestimate the cost of necessary renovations. Fixing and flipping are therefore best suited to people with in-depth knowledge of determining the fair market value of a house, the actual cost of improvements, and enough funds to complete the project on schedule and under budget.

Wholesaling real estate is another.
A version of fixing and flipping, real estate wholesaling is an investment technique where no wholesaler ever takes possession of the property. Instead, a real estate wholesaler looks for a distressed property with a motivated seller, puts the house under contract at a discount, determines what repairs are necessary and the home's final fair market value, and then assigns the purchase and sale agreement to another investor in exchange for a small wholesale fee. Similar to mending and flipping,

successful real estate wholesaling calls for a lot of time, in-depth market knowledge, and strong bargaining abilities to persuade a seller to accept less money than the property is worth. A property wholesaler also needs a license, which is required in several states.

For those who don't have a lot of money to invest, nevertheless, real estate wholesaling might be a wise course of action. Some seasoned real estate wholesalers employ "real estate bird dogs" to find the distressed property, and when the property is located, they give the bird dog a tiny referral fee.

7. REIGs

Small funds known as real estate investment groups (REIGs) buy collections of rental properties and then make those properties available for sale to investors. The REIG handles renting out vacant homes, finding tenants, collecting rent, managing the property, and doing upkeep in return for a portion of the monthly rental money.

Real estate investment tips

Investors in a REIG profit from their portions of any ongoing rental revenue and equity growth when the group's residences are sold. It's important to examine management and their prior record of success or failure before choosing a REIG if you're seeking a hands-off real estate investing plan.

8. REITs

Residential build-to-rent (BTR) subdivisions, commercial real estate, or special-use properties like data centers and cold storage facilities are all types of real estate assets that real estate investment trusts (REITs), which can be publicly or privately held, invest in. At least 90% of REITs' income must be distributed to shareholders in the form of dividends. They can be a useful tool for diversifying an investment portfolio so that you can make money from real estate without actually owning any property. Investment-grade buildings owned by a REIT are typically leased on long-term terms to credit tenants. Publicly listed REITs have shares that may be purchased or sold on an exchange, making them more liquid than conventional real estate investments. The advantages of directly owning a rental property, such as having direct influence over property management decisions, are not offered by REITs.

9. Crowdfunding.
Crowdfunding platforms are online real estate investment venues where investors pool funds to buy stakes in premium commercial and residential assets like newly constructed homes, apartment complexes, and stable commercial real estate. Crowdfunding can be a fantastic method to get exposure to properties that are out of reach for most investors to buy outright. If a project is lucrative, crowdfund investors will get regular pro-rata distributions of net income in addition to a cut of any profits made when a project is sold. Shares

frequently have lockup periods until a project is stable or during times of economic uncertainty, which is one of the negatives of crowdfunding. Shares also tend to be illiquid. Investors must rely on the crowdfund sponsor's expertise to find lucrative possibilities, finance and develop the project, then lease and manage the property to increase asset value and cash flow.

10. Personal loans

Instead of equity, private lenders engage in real estate debt. Private lenders provide loans to real estate investors looking for an alternative to conventional financing sources, such as home flippers, as opposed to investing themselves in rental property. Private lenders profit from lending fees and interest rates just like a conventional bank does. But costs and interest rates are typically greater.

However, there is a chance that a borrower would default, forcing a private lender to take back a property that has only been partially rehabilitated. Private lending may be a useful strategy to produce recurring interest revenue. For this reason, private lenders have their real estate investing experience and are aware of how to protect themselves if a property needs to be foreclosed.

Chapter 6

Making Your Business Stronger

With millions of licensed real estate agents already working in the country, real estate is a congested market. This can make it seem impossible to expand your business—"How am I ever going to outcompete all the agents I saw at that networking event the other night with my little business?"—and you may start to doubt your ability to do so. The good news is that you have the power to grow. You can engage in a range of activities to actively develop your company, attracting new customers and increasing sales along the way.

Real estate investment tips

You may find a list of the methods and strategies real estate brokers do below to increase their present income or generate more. We're confident there are at least a few you'll find helpful, from becoming a broker to flipping homes.

1. Repair and replace it

Perhaps you shouldn't buy a house that requires this much repair. A home that requires so many repairs might not be something you want to buy. You've thought about "flipping" a house if you've thought about purchasing, improving, and then selling a home. To provide an additional revenue stream, many real estate brokers turn to house flipping or assist clients in doing so. Contrary to what you might see on television, it's uncommon to make $100,000 on a flip. Flipping numerous houses for a small profit is where the real money is to be found, not in one massive flip.

Real estate investment tips

Flipping houses comes with a lot of danger as well. This tactic only works if you purchase a home below market value and have a precise idea of how much repairs will cost. Experience is crucial. Make sure you understand the after-repair value of a property before you purchase it (ARV). Although you'll likely need a real estate agent's assistance to determine this, you may get a general sense by looking at the most recent sales prices of homes in the same neighborhood. Of course, you're not required to make repairs to the house. Another option is to purchase at a discount and then sell as soon as feasible. Step two is important to note before you get into house flipping.

2. Look for unlisted, off-market properties
You'll have a difficult time making money if you can't find bargains before everyone else. Many of the homes that may bring in money for you are not listed on popular websites like MLS or Zillow. They aren't always

foreclosures; rather, they are the ones the owner needs to sell immediately.

An off-market property, often known as a "pocket listing," may be owned by a divorcing spouse or by a homeowner who no longer desires it for various reasons, such as financial difficulties or impending departure from the country. The owners of these homes typically can't sell them through conventional means because they need to sell quickly. They are the homes that you might pass while driving that has a sign that reads "For Sale by Owner" on the front. Your gems are those. You have a much better chance of buying a house below market value if you can find someone who needs money now. The highest return on your investment will come from these properties.

Keep an eye out for off-market houses by keeping a keen ear to the ground. You never know when a member of your network of

Real estate investment tips

friends, acquaintances, or family members will ask you for assistance on their behalf or on behalf of someone they know. publicize your name. Become a member of networks like Business Network International and the Rotary Club. In this manner, if someone in your network encounters a problem, they will think of you first! Try to network with estate attorneys in addition to your regular contacts. Their creditors frequently require quick access to funds. They will therefore be far more likely to sell for less. Making connections with wholesalers is also a smart idea because they frequently buy cheap properties that need work nearly as soon as they become available and turn a profit by selling them a few days later. They're playing the short game, so if you like the long game, this can be a beneficial tactic for you.

Visit Auction.com if you feel confident bidding on real estate. This website lets you look for both residential and commercial real estate. Because they have entered foreclosure or are bank-owned, many of the properties have low asking prices and are advertised on the website.

3. Focus on the vacation rental industry
Let's speak about how holiday rentals can help you make money or can assist your clients to make money. Owning a home you can rent to visitors during the busiest travel season may seem like a no-brainer decision—you create equity in a prime location and have the chance to profit from that demand. But what occurs after the peak travel period? If you've set the price of your rental too high, you'll likely experience a slow or at least unreliable off-season. The cost of all those vacancies will add up, especially if you have a property manager on staff. The true cost of a vacation rental is what it costs to manage and maintain it.

Pricing the home affordably so that it remains rented all year long is essential for a successful vacation rental. If you can't do that, you must make sure you have enough money during the good season. Despite cash flow issues, the vacation rental industry can still be a fantastic investment. A vacation rental website, Home Away, reports that the typical homeowner on their site leases his property for 18 weeks of the year (about four months), bringing in $28,000 yearly. That covers 75% of these property owners' annual mortgage payments, which is a wonderful long-term investment for them. Thoughtfully consider the ongoing costs of management, maintenance, and repairs before diving headfirst into this sector. Are you capable of doing this, or are you able to assist your clients in evaluating the needs and risks to maximize their ROI?

4. Beautify the home you're selling.
A lot of individuals find viewing a property to be an emotionally charged event. They have to envision what their life would be like if they were to reside there. You can have

trouble selling an empty house if you put it up for sale. The majority of clients make decisions about a home as soon as they see it. You could not be creating that powerful first impression, which is essential to pushing things along if the house you're selling simply includes pictures of vacant rooms. Nearly everyone who is looking for a home starts their search online, according to research from the National Association of Realtors. You might think about staging the house in this situation to make it appear occupied.

For a good reason, staging is popular: Houses staged by an Accredited Staging Professional (ASP®) sell in 33 days on average as opposed to 196 days for homes that are not staged. Therefore, if you're having trouble selling an empty property, think about putting in furniture to give the prospective buyer a better image of what this house looks like lived in, even only for the initial photo shoot!

5. Produce leads by sending direct mailers
Even if you focus on your ideal target market, this time-tested strategy still works today. The ROI is the same as social media marketing. A 2017 Direct Marketing Association survey found that direct mail performs better than all digital media in terms of response rates. It has a very low cost-per-acquisition of roughly $19, which makes it extremely competitive. Not all direct marketing is created equal, and "format" has a significant impact on response rate:

5% response rate for oversized envelopes

The response rate for postcards: is 4.25 percent

Dimensional: 4% response percentage

The response rate to catalogs: 3.9 percent

Real estate investment tips

3.5% of those who received letter-sized envelopes responded.

Direct mail's sole drawback is how tough it is to trace where leads are originating from or where they are first seeing you. Nevertheless, there are methods of tracking direct mail that can require a little bit more work or a little bit more money.Using direct mail to target clients is becoming less common, according to the same report. It follows that you have the chance to stand out and draw attention from the very beginning.

6. Complete the broker's exam
All you need to do to become a licensed real estate agent is pass the tests that your state specifies. You can sell real estate as an individual real estate agent or as an employee of a larger company after completing this process, which often takes no longer than a few months. However, most states mandate that new agents must

complete two years of apprenticeship under an experienced broker. The only thing you cannot do with this license starts your own business and recruit more real estate brokers. You need to become a broker to achieve it.

The broker's exam must be taken and passed before you can open your real estate brokerage and start paying commissions to the agents who work there. It pays to become your broker since you won't be losing out on the money you earn because most brokers take between 20 and 50 percent of an agent's commission. This is true even if you don't make any extra money.

Create your brand.

Developing your real estate brand is a crucial step in ensuring your long-term success. While most agents start their careers by investing in their broker's reputation, they discover that as time goes on and they consider switching brokers, things become much more challenging and it nearly feels like beginning again. You may make your business transitory so that you won't have to start from scratch if you decide to move to a new office by investing in your brand as a realtor. So where do you even start? Use these seven steps to launch the development of your real estate brand right away.

1. Establish Your Brand.
What attributes make up a strong personal brand? Finding your unique strengths is the first step. What makes you different from a rival? You might have years of expertise, specializing in working with buyers or sellers, have experience working with first-time homebuyers, know how to use a certain kind of loan application, or simply enjoy working with animals. When branding your real estate business, all of these things produce an abundance of chances for clients

to recognize and choose you as the person they want to work with.

2. Consider Your Audience

You should consider your target before beginning to market yourself in real estate. Does your marketing fit the kind of people you were attempting to reach? What are some of the problems that your clients have, for instance? How can you get in touch with these customers? While traditional phone conversations may be preferred by some people, text messaging is the most efficient form of communication for other groups of people. When developing your brand, it's critical to comprehend what motivates your target audience.

3. Make Yourself Stand Out Against Your Competition.

With constant rivalry, the real estate market is rising. Even though it can be daunting, developing your brand depends on knowing what your competitors are doing and being able to outperform them. You may often draw some lines based on how your rivals are reaching the audience you're also attempting to reach in your real estate market, which can help you become more noticeable and influential.

4. Take Small, Realistic Steps.
To achieve your broader objectives in your real estate business plan, you should start small and take concrete measures. If you have a name that people remember, they will call you first when they are ready to buy or list a house for sale. You may start developing your real estate brand by following these simple steps.

Make a logo for your company that accurately represents it. It may be inclusive of the region or the message that you were attempting to communicate to your target audience.

Build a website for yourself. Instead of being a digital extension of your broker, this website should be distinctive in how it markets you as a real estate agent. If you choose to quit that office, you won't be able to take your broker's website with you for the same reason that was previously mentioned.

Spend money on marketing initiatives. To effectively reach your audience, you must run digital, print, and community-focused ads.

5. Integrate photos and videos into your branding

Recognize the importance of photography and video storytelling when deciding how to build a real estate brand. When marketing a house, it's important to create a narrative in that purchasers can envision themselves living. When they see the backyard, you want them to picture having barbecues there with their loved ones. You want people to visualize their loved ones gathered around a Christmas tree for the season. You want them to watch as their kids grow up there. The images you select should be appealing and adaptable enough for anyone to look at them and see themselves living there with their family to realize this vision.

6. Avoid isolating your clients by being overly specialized.

The same is true when it comes to branding your real estate company. Make sure the material you use to promote your brand does not prevent you from dealing with certain clients. Avoid the chance of luring a potential customer just to have them turn away because they believe your highly specialized branding excludes them from your ability to assist them. If you claim to be an expert listing agent, it is a fantastic example of this. Do you want to brand yourself so strongly that someone looking to buy a house thinks they can't contact you for help because you only support sellers?

7. Make Your Brand Memorable
People work in the real estate industry. In other words, it all comes down to developing relationships over time so that people think of you first when they're ready to purchase or sell a home. Your branding needs to be memorable if you want to succeed in a cutthroat industry. You will struggle to maintain your position as a thought leader if your branding is identical to that of others or is simply so simple as to be quickly forgotten. Since people will eventually forget that you are even a real estate professional, this ultimately means that you will miss out on possibilities. The contrary is also true; you don't want your branding to be so outrageous that people think they can't take you seriously.